iam iwish ican

steffan soule

art by barbara halliday

isbn 978-1-942426-00-4
paperback color version 1.2

library of congress 2016920670

also in enhanced ebook format
isbn 978-1-942426-01-1

These pages contain sections-of-text which are whole images containing meaning. The form of the page and their sequence create an effect on our inner reading.

The intent is to read with our deeper mind, our whole mind and our subconsciousness.

Reading in this way brings these ideas into our true nature where they become much more than information or knowledge.

Another way of putting this is "Turn to the next page only when you connect fully with the ideas on the page you're on."

i am

i wish

i can

Three sacred impulses,

already in you,

awaiting your call.

Impulses that connect you with the authentic power to choose your life and create your world.

You increase the power
of *I am, I wish,* and *I can*
inside you
with relaxation,
imagination
and repetition.

As this power increases, you attract your dreams, manifest your heart's desire, and bring your true self into every meaningful relationship.

You enter into the causative level of your life where you can create what you imagine.

By activating these impulses,
you engender a
higher level of creativity
that is a definite possibility
for a human being.

By now you already recognize that positive, creative, higher impulses need to be encouraged and cultivated

because many of our automatic impulses destroy things.

To become, and live by
our true selves,
a special effort
to develop inner capacities
is needed.

But how?

This way of iamiwishican
prepares us for making those efforts.
This way provides a direct connection to
how.

How to develop positive impulses, ideas,
values, images, and creativity.

Keep in mind that effort can be receptive as well as active.

A receptive effort allows ideas, values, and images of higher degrees of reason to enter into existence—through us and into our lives. Active efforts of choice and receptive efforts with deep relaxation are both necessary. It is important that the word "effort" be understood in this way, that it includes our receptivity.

Let's begin again with

i am

say it...

...inwardly

i am

And in the silence issuing from your
intonation of this sacred impulse,
your presence and your being grow
deeper and
more harmonious.

In the quiet inner state
that accompanies
each one of your
three sacred impulses,
special meaning emerges

...over time, with
repetition.

In the quiet receptivity
that accompanies
these sacred impulses...

...the power to see into the present moment and receive meaningful insights becomes available.

The power to "see into" is about seeing. It's the power to see, feel, image, sense, to fully experience, grok, etc...

Now, with this meaning in mind, we repeat the previous two ideas, together:

In the quiet receptivity
that accompanies
these sacred impulses...

...the power to see into the
present moment and receive
meaningful insights
becomes available.

The experience of seeing along with your insights becomes your own understanding.

This serves as your guide while you become your true self and create what you intend.

We will come back to quiet inner work later
on, and we will also show how to work—just
as effectively—in a noisy cafe,
or anywhere at all, but right now,

our further explorations require words,
which is not exactly the same
as silence or a quiet inner state.

To boost the meaning and significance
that you get from
these three sacred impulses,
and to develop your capacity to
utilize them for the growth of your
inner life, that is your being,

we will explore special, powerful ideas
right here, right now.

You see, relaxing and repeating the phrases that represent the three sacred impulses is necessary but not sufficient.

We need the addition of the specific, powerful ideas that follow because... they help.

Ideas from a higher, refined degree of reason, of wisdom, offer a particular kind of help to us. Fortunately, they are simple and accessible.

Just by *reading*, repeating ↻ or even picturing ∞
these special ideas,
you will begin to absorb them into your
subconscious.

This brings them closer to
your understanding....

You will not need to think about them
in order for them to have their
beneficial effect.

So let's get to work.

i am

Now is a new present moment.
I am here, fully present in this place,
in this body, in this life.
I am here now and I have the right
to be here. I am alive.

i
am

And I have three questions for you to consider...

What is your destiny?

Who are you?

How are you going to get there?

I know the answer to two of them:

I already know who you are; and I know what your destiny is.

You also know, deep down.

So we can say that
we know who you are, and
we know what your destiny is.

I don't know
how you will get there.

And although I don't know

the details of how you will get there, as you engage, activate & cultivate *I Am, I Wish, I Can*, you will get there. You will intentionally actualize your destiny.

What you want is connected with your destiny.

When we speak of your destiny, we include what you want, your heart's desire, the love of your life.

What you want is important.

This is not about your egoistic aims or your likes and dislikes.

Asking for more of that will only
take you deeper into your fate.

Some live only by fate.
You reach beyond fate.
For example, you found
iamiwishican which leads you
toward manifesting your heart's
desire.

What is your Destiny?

What do you love to do, and how do you wish to give?

What you love is important. What you love to do, what activates your love and what you want to give

all relate to wish.

i wish

i wish

I sense the impulse of *I wish* inside my being.

i wish

I do not focus my wish on anything
that I want.
Instead, I sense the presence
inside of pure wish.

i wish

without a need to
fill in the blank,
without limiting the impulse of wish
by ending the sentence...

The sentence does go on however, after the pure impulse is clearly present.

i wish

I wish to be (present here and now)...
wish for higher being (my highest self to be in my life)...
wish to give (to others) without limits...

i wish

Not for any
thing;
I sense the pure power of
unassigned, unattached wish.

The naked, sacred impulse itself.

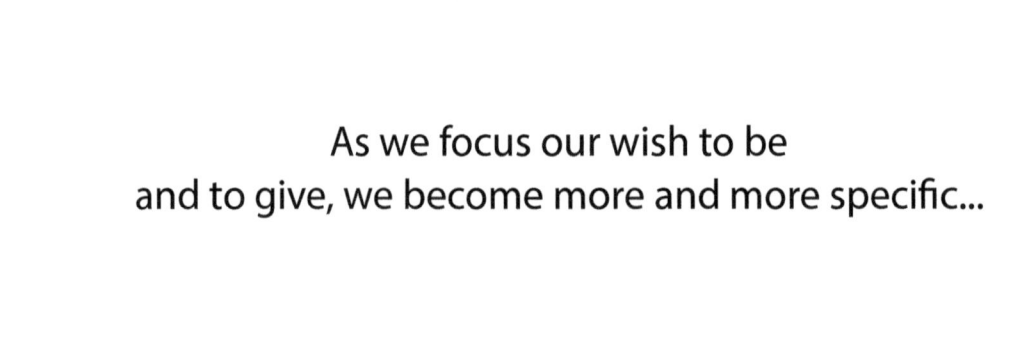

As we focus our wish to be
and to give, we become more and more specific...

i wish

I want to give from my essence.

The music of my soul
is for the world, and I want to play it.

I want to give it.

i
wish

I wish to be, I wish to give.

I am, I wish

I am present as my heart reaches up and out with a wish to give.

i am here, now, in the present
moment.
i wish to give.

But, the third question remains in full force: how will you get there?

i can holds the key..., but let's go back before we go forward.

Now that you have a sense for the first two impulses that are proper for you to have enlivened, bring your attention back to the question...

Who am I?

The first word in each of our three statements—this one letter word "I"—must mean something.

Who are you?

Can you sense your true self?
Your sense of "I", inside you, reveals an illusion.

Who are you really? Beyond the pictures you have built up, beyond personality? Reach into your essence....

Can you think about your self...
                                ...without naming what you do?
Can you feel that you are divine?

With these questions in mind, we will now connect with a statement of identity that comes from antiquity.

First we will include the word "God." Later we will connect the same idea without that word, because

some of us need different ways—or both ways—of stating these ideas.

You are a child of God. You are godlike.

You have the same possibilities and the same impossibilities as God has, the difference being only in scale.

Fortunately for you, you are not God for the whole wide world. That's too large a scale.

But, you can be God for your world.

And this includes your inner world.

How thoroughly have you explored and organized your inner world?

We put lots of attention on mastering the outer world, yet we can learn infinitely more about the inner world.

Your inner world will become more unified—able to create—as you work with what comes to you and reverberates through the sacred impulses
I Am I Wish I Can.

These three phrases are shortcuts
for meaningful, purposeful pathways
that you already have but
must cultivate.

So let's go back to what we know already... deep down, ...about you.

We know who you are: You are a child of God; you are godlike. You are in the image of God.

And we know your destiny: to give.

You are a giver, and as with many givers, there is sometimes the danger that you may give too much, so please accept this gentle reminder that you must also give to yourself.

In order to give most effectively, most efficiently, you must care for yourself.

Whatever you need, whatever you may require in order to be able to give, you can have, provided that you use it to give to others,

to maintain and continue a beautiful balance of harmony and love between yourself and others.

Giving to self and others is described in the Golden Rule which is a common cosmic law, a universal principle that we utilize through attention, practice and repetition.

Empathy is built into our human biology. In every society and culture we find unique expressions of the Golden Rule.

Each of these thousands of ways shows us *how* to be kind, open, and giving to others even when it is difficult.

Seeing many expressions of the Golden Rule together can make quite an impression.

"There is no better training in awareness and sensitivity~even understanding and attention~because in order to consider my brother or my neighbor externally I need to take him or her into the field of my attention in a very real way. I must be open to his or her needs, sufferings, and that means putting some of my own self-absorbtion off to one side." — **Annie Lou Stavely**

"Don't go around hurting people and try to understand things." — **Capo 2nd Hopi Indian Culture**

"You shall love your neighbor as yourself." Judeo-Christian — **Leviticus 19:18**

"The heart of the person before you is a mirror. See there your own form." — **Shinto**

"What you would avoid suffering yourself, seek not to impose upon others." Greek Philosopher — **Epictetus**

"One should seek for others the happiness one desires for one's self." — **Buddhist**

"Nations must treat other nations as they wish to be treated. Thus, peace." — **Jonathan Granoff**

"No one of you is a believer until he desires for his brother that which he desires for himself." — **Islam**

"The golden way was to be friends with the world and to regard the whole family like the members of one family." — **Mahatma Gandhi**

"It is a very high goal: free and responsible development of the individual, so that he may place his powers freely and gladly in the service of mankind." — **Albert Einstein**

African "One going to take a pointed stick to pinch a baby bird should first try it on himself to feel how it hurts." Yoruba Proverb African Traditional (Nigeria)
Bahá'i "Blessed is he who preferreth his brother before himself." Bahá'u'lláh, Tablets of Bahá'u'lláh "Hurt not others in ways that you yourself would find hurtful." **Buddhism** "All beings love life. All beings fear death. Knowing this the wise man does not kill nor cause to kill." Dhammapadha **Christianity** "Therefore, whatever you want men to do to you, do also to them, for this is the Law and the Prophets." Yahshua, Matthew 7:12 "Kind words can be short and easy to speak, but their echoes are truly endless." - Mother Theresa "We cannot all do great things, but we can do small things with great love." - Mother Theresa **Confucianism** "Do not do to others what you would not like yourself. Then there will be no resentment against you, either in the family or in the state." Analects 12:2 "Try your best to treat others as you would wish to be treated yourself, and you will find that this is the shortest way to benevolence." Mencius VII.A.4 **Greek Philosophers** "We should behave to friends as we would wish friends to behave to us." Aristotle "Do not do to others what would anger you if done to you by others." or "Do not do to others that which would anger you if others did it to you." Socrates "What you would avoid suffering yourself, seek not to impose upon others." Epictetus **The Gurdjieff Work** "I am Thou Thou are I He is ours We both are His So may all be for our neighbor." "Only he can be just who is able to put himself in the position of others. Only he who can take care of what belongs to others may have his own. Treat Another's as your own and be ye so related." "The highest aim and sense of human life is the striving to attain the welfare of one's neighbor," and that this is possible exclusively only by the conscious renunciation of one's own. G.I. Gurdjieff **Hinduism** "This is the sum of duty; do naught onto others what you would not have them do unto you." Mahabharata "One should not behave towards others in a way which is disagreeable to oneself. This is the essence of morality. All

other activities are due to selfish desire." Mahabharata, Anusasana Parva 113.8
Humanism "Humanists acknowledge human interdependence, the need for mutual respect and the kinship of all humanity. Humanists affirm that individual and social problems can only be resolved by means of human reason, intelligent effort, critical thinking joined with compassion and a spirit of empathy for all living beings. " **Individuals** "Be the change you wish to see in the world." - Gandhi "No act of kindness, no matter how small, is ever wasted." - Aesop "Wherever there is a human being, there is an opportunity for kindness." - Seneca "It is when you give of yourself that you truly give." - Kahil Gibran "Kindness is the golden chain by which society is bound together." - Goethe "Do not wait for leaders; do it alone, person to person." - Mother Theresa "What wisdom can you find that is greater than kindness?" - Rousseau "Every man takes care that his neighbor does not cheat him. But the day comes when he begins to care that he does not cheat his neighbor. Then all goes well." - Ralph Waldo Emerson "The Golden Rule would reconcile capital and labor, all political contention and uproar, all selfishness and greed." Joseph Parker "We need to feel the problems of others as our own. . ." Rigoberta Menchu´ Tum, a woman from Guatemala and Nobel Peace Prize recipient. "As we try living by the golden rule, treating everyone as we would like to be treated, we find that it is an ongoing process, not to be achieved in one day, but hopefully in a lifetime." Dolly Larsen **Islam** "Not one of you truly believes until you wish for others that which you wish for yourself." The Prophet Mohammed **Jainism** "In happiness and suffering, in joy and grief, we should regard all creatures as we regard our own self." Lord Mahavir 24th Tirthankara "One should treat all beings as he himself would be treated." Agamas Sutrakritanga 1.10.13 **Judaism** "You shall not take vengeance, nor bear any grudge against the children of your people, but you shall love your neighbor as yourself: I am the LORD." YHWH, Leviticus 19:18 **Latter-Day Saints** "And let every man esteem his brother as himself, and practice

virtue and holiness before me." -Doctrine and Covenants 38:24 **Native American** "Respect for all life is the foundation." The Great Law of Peace "All things are our relatives; what we do to everything, we do to ourselves. All is really One." Black Elk "Whatever befalls the earth, befalls the sons of the earth. Man did not weave the web of life; he is merely a strand in it. Whatever he does to the web, he does to himself. " Chief Seattle **Persian** "Do as you would be done by." **Roman Antiquity** "Treat your inferiors as you would be treated by your superiors." Seneca: Epistle 47:11 "The law imprinted on the hearts of all men is to love the members of society as themselves." Roman Pagan Religion. **Shintoism** Be charitable to all beings, love is the representative of God. Ko-ji-ki Hachiman Kasuga "The heart of the person before you is a mirror. See there your own form" Shinto: **Sikhism** "Do not create enmity with anyone as God is within everyone." Guru Arjan Devji 259. "Compassion-mercy and religion are the support of the entire world". Japji Sahib **Sufism** "The basis of Sufism is consideration of the hearts and feelings of others. If you haven't the will to gladden someone's heart, then at least beware lest you hurt someone's heart, for on our path, no sin exists but this." Dr. Javad Nurbakhsh, Master of the Nimatullahi Sufi Order. **Taoism** "Regard your neighbor's gain as your gain, and your neighbor's loss as your own loss." Tai Shang Kan Yin P'ien "To those who are good to me, I am good; to those who are not good to me, I am also good. Thus all get to be good. To those who are sincere with me, I am sincere; to those who are not sincere with me, I am also sincere. Thus all get to be sincere." **Utilitarianism** "To do as one would be done by, and to love one's neighbor as one's self, constitute the ideal perfection of utilitarian morality." John Stuart Mill **Unitarianism** "We affirm and promote respect for the interdependent of all existence of which we are a part." Unitarian principles. **Zoroastrianism** "That nature alone is good which refrains from doing to another whatsoever is not good for itself." Dadisten-I-dinik, 94,5   more at: **goldenruleproject.org**

Recognize that each expression of this wise and universal principle describes self and other in a reciprocal relationship.

In order to maintain a balance of harmony and love with self and other, we strive to care for ourselves and others *simultaneously*. Joy increases and sorrow decreases as we engage the reciprocity of the Golden Rule which is giving.

Giving is the destiny of every being. The question is whether a being chooses to give, and intentionally joins the creative process, or whether a being gives only automatically—such as at death when the body returns to the earth.

The three sacred impulses of I Am, I Wish, I Can relate with the reality *and the quality* of giving.

I Am is an abbreviation for a large idea. The meaning of I Am deepens with experience. When you say "I Am," expand your meaning of I Am to include:

"I am a child of God. I am godlike. God is unknowable. I am unknowable."

And to say this without using the word God:

"I am a child of the Universe. I am in the pattern of natural, physical, universal laws. These laws are not all knowable. I am unknowable."

And what is relevant about being unknowable?

Knowledge has limits. We know we have limits, but we do not know the extent of our limits, not entirely.

Not knowing leads us to be open to imagining even the impossible (which actually might be possible). The use of free and open imagination coupled with presence and attention is partly how our positive wishes and dreams become reality.

Naturally a healthy sense of detachment arises in us when we include the idea that "I am unknowable." A simple statement of detachment is:

I am I
I am not that

Imagine: I am... *the identity we have been defining (your expanded meaning of I Am)*, and I am not... *the external world or reactive inner world*. I am... *the real (unknowable, unconditioned) I*, and I am not... *the conditioned world that catches my attention and "makes me" think, feel, sense that I am those conditions*. As you work with that phrase above and repeat it in many situations, you will see it is true (law conformable), and that most problems result from cases of mistaken identity.

Recognizing your true identity with detachment accelerates manifesting your wishes because it opens you up to infinite potential.

Detachment is the practice of being and becoming your true identity.

We will return to the importance of detachment once we understand more about the natural, physical, universal laws in which we find ourselves and the creative impulse of "I Can."

i can

There is a specific teaching of "i can." It is designed to boost the creative powers in the recipient—which is you.

There is not one historical source to credit for this teaching. We can appreciate this as a new source and remember that these ideas come to us through many lines and from all directions at all times.

There exists a special teaching of "i can," and it is revealed here in full form and splendid sequence. This is "special" because it contains *all* of what is required for the full actualization of this popular "secret"...

...and it comes from a refined degree of reason of understanding.

See the end credits for references pointing to the origins of this teaching.

i can

This impulse connects with our imagination and with our physical ability to act. It relates to faith and holds a key to becoming a genuine being who can serve, give and create.

i can

I may be formed in the likeness of universal laws and my destiny may actually revolve around giving, but... how?

In order to live according to my potential, the impulse of "I can" enters into my common presence, and I act with a willingness to
                        become,
                      to create,
                       to give,
                    to serve others.

But what do I want to create? And how do I manifest
and receive what I wish to give
such that
it becomes
reality?

"I can" includes the big idea:

"I can create anything I imagine within the constraints of natural, physical, universal laws."

When you imagine a desired future event; when you imagine a creation, something you want to make, do or create, you are forming a plan. And this plan is a statement of faith because it deals with the unknowable.

The future is unknowable.

We do not know everything about the natural, physical, universal laws that influence us or our future. We do not know all of them. We do know some of them. We make plans based upon our limited knowledge of the future and what we want to create.

Therefore a plan is a statement of faith because it utilizes the future which is unknowable.

A plan is a *knowable* expression of faith, a way to work with the unknowable.

Here the word faith refers to the marvelous faculty with which everyone is equipped and it does not, in this case, refer to religion.

What this faculty of faith provides and how it pertains to "i can" will soon become clear.

Faith is a faculty with which you were born, and it allows you to deal with, to process, to accept

the unknowable.

When speaking about faith, we are talking about a property that is inherent in all people. Religious faith is an entirely different topic*.

*We are naming and viewing faith from an impartial perspective, before it connects with beliefs and becomes patterned with any particular content.

There are four aspects of faith in human life.

The first aspect gives you the ability to accept without empirical proof. This enables learning and the expansion of consciousness.

Faith develops in you soon after you take your first breath. It grows in people along with consciousness. You accept what you are told when you are a baby, and you begin to learn from those responsible for your education. We can call these responsible beings Mommy and Daddy for simplicity.

Faith grows as consciousness expands. When your mommy tells you, "You are my child; this is Daddy, I am your Mommy; this is red, and this is blue" you believe this without proof.

Learning begins with faith. We naturally accept what we are told while we grow up, and through repetition, learning with acceptance becomes part of our everyday life.

This allows our consciousness and our understanding to grow and expand. Without faith, nothing would happen!

The second aspect of faith gives you the ability to accept and work with the unknowable. Infinity, absolute, God, the soul and the future are all unknowable.

We do not know the future or infinity. We do not know gravity, endlessness, the Absolute, God, the soul. All these are unknowable.

Religion and philosophy help us relate with unknowable God and unknowable soul.

Advanced mathematics relies on relating with the unknowable concepts of infinity and the absolute. Without advanced mathematics our progress would be very slow. We'd still be in the stone age.

Without a way to relate with the unknowable, we would be stuck.

The third aspect of your faith gives you instant access to the realm of extra sensory faculties: intuition, premonition, precognition, mind to mind communication.

This aspect of faith is subjective. We have flashes of understanding and can know things by intuition on occasion but not constantly.

The fourth aspect of your faith is the creative, causative aspect. It works only when the intensity of your belief reaches the level of conviction.

When what you want to happen or what you believe is going to happen feels as though you knew darn well that it was going to happen, then you enter into the causative mode in which you can cause future events without any apparent physical involvement.

Simply imagine the desired future event or events. Provided what you imagine conforms to the universal, natural, physical laws, the desired future events take place as scheduled.

This idea is worth repeating.

When you reach the fourth aspect of faith, you enter the causative level in which what you believe will happen feels and seems as though it has already happened.

This is the level of conviction where what you believe—what you imagine is going to happen—takes place as if you knew it was going to happen.

You are convinced it will happen, and your conviction seems to cause the future desired event to take place without any apparent physical involvement.*

*see "brain waves" pg 186. There probably is physical involvement. It is currently invisible and without measure. Neuroscience offers theoretical, yet reasonable, explanations.

Once you reach the causative level of faith, you manifest what you imagine on a regular basis.

To get there requires positive use of imagination, relaxation and repetition.

And it requires a plan, a vision of what you want to create.

To plan, first you dream. . .

and dream big.

Let yourself go!

Put your ideas on paper and imagine anything you want. Write down what you want, what you love, and if this is difficult, repeat the effort until something comes.

Then focus your dreams into a life plan.

You can change your life plan anytime, but for a complete and meaningful picture, be sure your plan addresses these five areas: career, personal-family, spiritual, cultural, community involvement.

By placing your ideas on paper, you strengthen your ability to visualize what you want and you integrate your dreams with your plans. You clarify your intentions. Visualizing your intentions with clarity and without fear helps you bring your dreams into reality.

Putting a plan on paper also assists with detachment. This is one of the key factors for success when applying the causative aspect of faith.

With detachment, the process evolves and involves with greatest efficiency. The statement "I am I, I am not that" helps you connect with your real self (I) while avoiding getting caught up in the results (that).

Looking at plans on paper helps you see and imagine the results with detachment.

All dreams are shared dreams. Even leaders who present a big dream that others follow begin with a common vision. When your dreams come true, others' dreams come true too.

Becoming sensitive to what you want, what you wish for, what you are passionate about is important. With this sensitivity, your dreams naturally emerge. What are you passionate about?

When you experience the sacred impulse wish, you connect with your destiny to give, and ideas, images or dreams arise in your consciousness for what you will become and what you want to do.

As you connect with your sacred impulse wish, hope builds. Hope, which is now also in your consciousness, leads to a natural unfolding into the world of "I can."

Our shared meaning of I Can has developed throughout our descriptions. It is now packed with significance.

This phrase I Can is short for our statement of creativity: "I can create anything I imagine within the constraints of natural, physical, universal laws."

In addition, this phrase represents one of our three sacred impulses, and its meaning includes our statement of identity, of "I."

It is possible to connect with all of this (the entire shared meaning of I Can) simultaneously, in your attention while you inwardly intone "i can."

i can

This phrase can be unpacked with your attention. It can not be done by reciting an exact series of words. Silent, quiet presence helps to focus the attention.

With your free attention, you simultaneously breathe life into this impulse and boost the intensity of your belief.

To say I CAN inwardly, and sincerely from the true self, it helps to renew contact with I AM and with I WISH.

First, relax and direct your free attention into the present moment. Become your true identity (i am). Next, sense the power of pure wish, to give to the world, to bring qualities from the higher into the lower, from the unknowable into the knowable, from the invisible into the visible (i wish).

Now shift your attention to see I CAN.

Continue to maintain relaxation, as deeply as possible.

Call on the sacred impulse of I CAN.

Know that *you can create.*

Imagine your desired future event or events, and picture this clearly with as much detail as possible. You are receiving these images. Relaxation and receptivity lead you in this effort.

Inwardly intone

I CAN

Do this for as long as you feel comfortable. It helps to repeat this at the same time each day.

When you bring your exercise to a close, keep a connection with your intent and your belief.

In between these sessions, during ordinary life, you can inwardly repeat "I CAN" while maintaining contact with the full meaning of the phrase.

"I can" will become active as a sacred impulse. It is necessary to incorporate everything we have discussed, and then, it is necessary to let it all go and bathe in the presence of "I can" without filling in the blank.

Allow a sense of emptiness to accompany the moment after intoning the phrase that represents the sacred impulse. See if something emerges.

I CAN

Each of these sacred impulses causes a reverberation in a person with genuine presence. What does this actually mean? How can any phrase—inwardly intoned—cause a reverberation?

What must be in place for a reverberation to occur?

Can you relax, become quiet inside and intone these sacred impulses now with a new sense of who you are, what you are here for and how you will manifest your heart's desire, your true self, your destiny?

iam iwish ican

It may be useful to flip to the page that starts iamiwishican, and read this all again to see what comes.... These ideas work on us—just like the sacred impulses work within us.

This time you can deepen your sense of WE. It is important to work with the Golden Rule and relate to others as they are you. The self-other relationship is in everything. All of your dreams connect and manifest with others.

And then we can boost your faith to the causative level.

In order to utilize the fourth aspect of faith, in harmony with the sacred impulse of *I CAN*, you must boost your faith to the causative level.

Because it may be difficult to do this alone, there exist ways to boost your faith to help you experience the causative level.

The following is an inner exercise for boosting your faith to the causative level. There are many of these exercises for different stages and purposes. This one unifies everything we have discussed so far. You will receive this boost with an intensity equal to the gravity with which you have allowed these ideas to sink in up to this point.

In addition to the following text, links to audio of this exercise appear in all ebook versions of this book, and at iamiwishican.com/afe

Relax

Close your eyes. Take three deep breaths.

With each exhalation, your body relaxes instinctively, deeper and deeper.

Sense your body

Bring your attention into your entire body, all at once or part by part starting at the toes and drawing the attention and sensation up the body to the crown of the head.

Sensing the entire body and maintaining relaxation and presence, we begin with whole brain experiences that open us to the higher, sacred impulses.

Breathe in I

And exhale AM.

I—in breath: the air comes into the top of the head down the spine, and filling the lungs, it connects with the blood.

AM—out breath: the air flows out but the energy from the air permeates the whole body, all at once, and adds to the sensation of presence in the body.

Follow all this with your attention while intoning I AM.

Who am I?

As you breathe I—AM, you begin to open to the question.

Who am I?

And you detach from all answers. You hold the question. The unknowable I arises inside.

I wish

As you breathe in and out I—AM, and you ask "Who am I?", while you detach from the answer, you begin to feel a presence at the Center of the Chest.

Into this presence in the Center of the Chest, you inwardly intone, "I WISH." Breathe in I; breathe out Wish.

And here you feel the power of your true self having an honest and sincere wish—to be and to do—from a higher, creative level. There is no thing attached, only the pure impulse.

I can

Once you have contact with Am and Wish, you bring your attention to the center of your forehead and inwardly intone "I CAN."

On the in breath, you sense energy, like the energy in the air, coming into the center of the head, and you image "I," and with the out breath, you intone the impulse of "CAN."

I CAN at the center of the forehead.

While these three sacred impulses can be in any one of the three brains: body, feeling and mind, we place them in this way for this particular expression.

Sense all three at once.

I am I wish I can

Three sacred impulses,
awakened inside
your brains

Now picture your role—as a giver—and come back to I AM with the image of your role.

Breathe in I, sense the whole body on the out breath with AM.

And you finish this sentence with a simple, positive statement such as,
"I AM a great _____."

Once you have contact with this reality, move to the Center of your Chest and feel WISH.

Breathe in I and out WISH at the Center of the Chest as you now finish this sentence:

"I Wish to Give _____."

You finish these sentences with who you are (i am) and what you wish to be and give to the world (i wish).

Come to the center of the forehead, between the eyes and inside about an inch. Bring your attention there and activate the impulse of I CAN.

And as you breathe in and out with I CAN while sensing the forehead, you now finish this sentence by picturing what you want to create and by saying it inwardly,

"I CAN give _____ to the world."

Once you have contact with I CAN, bring your exercise to a close by slowly opening your eyes, moving your body and coming to a standing posture.

Give thanks.

Aim to serve.

Fini.

I am I wish I can

We don't know all of the universal, natural, physical laws. This work assists us to manifest results that are as close as possible to what the laws permit. Not everything happens just like we imagine. The laws may not conform to our exact picture. That is normal. We come close. We come closer than if we approach our aims haphazardly. And sometimes we exceed our dreams and apparently accomplish the impossible.

By repeating this exercise in a relaxed state with full presence, receptivity and detachment from results, you actualize your future desired event or events and cause them to manifest as if by magic.

But this is not magic. Your imagination blueprints your future. Here you learn to do this intentionally, for positive, life affirming reasons, and for purposes of giving-to-others.

Most people follow a blueprint that does not come from their own initiative. It takes intentional effort and receptivity to create your own blueprint.

You receive what you intend and you actualize your wishes because of repetition and perseverance—which brings your manifestations and impulses into alignment with the values that you have consciously set for yourself in order to achieve your aims.

This is "one of the laws," and while it's magical, it's not magic.

Brain waves...

One explanation which is important to consider (and ponder the significance) has to do with extremely low frequency waves or "ELF waves." It is likely, but not verified, that our imaging capacities (thinking, feeling, sensing) emit information through ELF waves that others can receive.

When we picture our desired future, regularly and with deep relaxation, our brain goes into the alpha state in which the brain emits ELF waves at approximately 8 Hz. This is the frequency that the military uses to communicate through the earth because it has low resistance and can travel with almost no impedance around the globe. Since our brains emit these ELF waves, the possibility exists that our images travel to those who would resonate with these images and help us with our aims.

Proof in results

The proof for how this teaching works—with its methods & ideas—is less important right now than our understanding that it does work.

As you engage the sacred impulses and the special ideas included in iamiwishican, you will find many ways to apply this teaching, and the results will be your proof. You can utilize this for strengthening your health, actualizing your dreams, manifesting your life plan, and for achieving success and prosperity in your profession and in love.

You will activate your true self and receive your desired, pictured, future events. And you will know it works by doing it, by the results.

Connect with your inner presence and attention and then use the keys.

The keys are relaxation,

repetition,

imagination

and boosting the intensity of your belief
to the level of conviction.

More to come...

Additional applications of these ideas and guided visualizations are available for download.

As you engage with iamiwishican and want to share your reflections, sign into the facebook page or the domain iamiwishican.com, and tell your story.

Share your insights and discover ways to engage and practice as we listen to our common experiences.

Thank you for your kindness, love and attention.

end credits—from the author
my mother and father taught us to repeat i can with visualization for many
purposes such as improving abilities or healing pain or headaches,
and it worked

my spiritual grandfather, gurdjieff, writes about three of seven sacred
impulses in his third series, and his insight is deep, his work essential

my raja yoga master friend, dr. gladych, transmitted the causative level of
faith and much more, one on one, for years, beautiful years

i quote from all of these remarkable people within this text and i choose
not to intrude on the reader by siting quotations
i believe each would approve of this choice and even instruct it

finally, my life experience is filled with examples of this practice in action
it is profound and serves as my direct connection to understanding
which leads me to embrace I and Thou:
we are, we wish, we can

I am I wish I can

by magician, author, speaker Steffan Soule

Presence, Destiny, and the power to Create
what you truly want.

Lightning Source UK Ltd.
Milton Keynes UK
UKHW050138010919
348817UK00003B/20/P